ANGLO-AMERICAN COLONIZATION

Richard Pickman

Rosen
Classroom™

New York

D1225843

Published in 2010 by The Rosen Publishing Group, Inc.
29 East 21st Street, New York, NY 10010

Book Design: Daniel Hosek

Photo Credits: Cover (wagon train), p. 5 © The Bridgeman Art Library/Getty Images; cover (Stephen Austin),
pp. 7, 11, 15 (Stephen Austin), 23, 24 courtesy Wikimedia Commons; cover (map back ground), pp. 17,
25 courtesy of Texas State Library and Archives Commission; interior borders and backgrounds, pp. 14–15,
28 Shutterstock; p. 6 © Jill Torrance/Getty Images; pp. 8, 9 © Geoatlas; p.10 © Joe Raedle/Getty Images;
p. 13 © Alfred Eisenstaedt/Time & Life Pictures/Getty Images; p. 19 courtesy Library of Congress; p. 21 ©
Hulton Archive/Getty Images; pp. 26, 27 The State Preservation Board, Austin, Texas.

Library of Congress Cataloging-in-Publication Data

Pickman, Richard.
Anglo-American colonization of Texas / Richard Pickman.
     p. cm. — (Spotlight on Texas)
Includes index.
ISBN 978-1-61532-462-0 (pbk.)
ISBN 978-1-61532-464-4 (library binding)
ISBN 978-1-65132-463-7 (6-pack)
1. Texas—History—To 1846—Juvenile literature. 2. Texas—Colonization—History—19th century—Juvenile
literature. 3. European Americans—Texas—History—19th century—Juvenile literature. I. Title.
F389.P535 2010
976.4′05—dc22

2009027286

Manufactured in the United States of America

CPSIA Compliance Information: Batch # WW10RC: For further information contact Rosen Publishing, New York, New York at 1-800-237-9932.

CONTENTS

MOVING TO TEXAS

Did you know the area today called Texas was once home to many different Native American groups? About 500 years ago, Spain claimed the area. Later it was part of Mexico. Anglo-American colonization between 1821 and 1835 finally led Texas to become a free country, then part of the United States.

An Anglo-American is an American who speaks English and whose family came from some part of Europe other than Spain. Around 1821, Anglo-Americans began settling in Texas. Before Anglo-American colonization, the non-Indian population of Texas was only about 3,000. By 1835, it had grown to about 35,000 people. Let's look at the reasons why Anglo-Americans settled in Texas and the effects it had on Texas, Mexico, and the United States.

Many Anglo-American settlers traveled to Texas in groups called wagon trains. They were sometimes attacked by Native Americans.

SPANISH TEXAS

During the 1500s and 1600s, Spanish **explorers** claimed present-day Mexico and the southwestern United States for Spain. They did this even though Native Americans had lived there for hundreds of years. They named the area New Spain.

Very few Spanish people settled in Texas at first. Soon, French explorers also showed an interest in this area. Spain feared France would try to claim the area and build settlements. So Spain decided to act first by building missions. Some of these missions grew into the first Spanish settlements in Texas. They created a starting point for future colonization.

The Alamo mission was the site of a historic battle during the Texas Revolution. Today, it's one of the most popular places in Texas for travelers to visit.

Spanish Missions in Texas

Missions were buildings that served as churches and community centers. Missions brought native and Spanish people together under Spanish rule and the **Catholic** faith. Spain hoped this would reduce fighting between the groups and increase the population of New Spain.

By the late 1700s, there were about thirty-seven missions in Texas. The most famous is San Antonio de Valero—better known as the Alamo. The missions often helped Spain found settlements in New Spain, but they weren't always successful. Anglo-Americans used some missions, such as the Alamo, as forts during the Texas **Revolution**.

Mission Concepción in San Antonio

In the early 1800s, the Spanish government wanted to keep others out of Texas. However, they had a hard time getting people in Mexico to move to the northern **frontier**. By 1820, there were only three settlements in Texas: Nacogdoches, San Antonio, and La Bahía (later called Goliad). They were very small towns surrounded by large ranches.

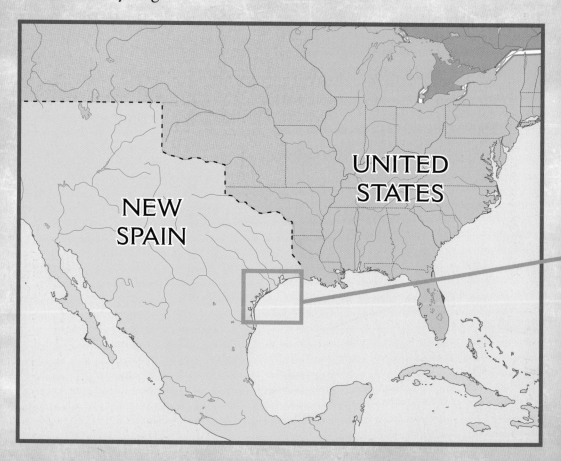

Native Americans were always trying to drive out the Spanish settlers. The Spanish government decided to invite outsiders to settle in what is now Texas. They hoped to stop the Indian attacks and strengthen the **economy** of Mexico. The Spanish government promised Anglo-American colonists cheap land, but they expected several things. Colonists were supposed to be Catholic, speak Spanish, and follow Spanish laws.

The Spanish government in Mexico offered Anglo-American colonists more than 4,500 acres per family for about 4 cents an acre. The government later reduced this price.

The Spanish government came up with a system to bring settlers to Texas quickly. They planned to give large areas of land to men they called empresarios (ehm-preh-SAHR-yohz). In return, the empresarios were expected to bring a certain number of settlers to Texas.

The empresarios were expected to set up communities for the settlers and uphold Mexican laws. They also decided where the colonists would set up their farms and homes. The land given to each colonist depended on the number of people in the family. Later, the size of land grants depended on the way it was to be used: for farming, ranching, or both. Settlers were free from paying taxes for 6 years. The more settlers an empresario brought to Texas, the more land he received for his own use.

definition
A man who was given a large amount of land in Texas by the Mexican government. In return, he promised to bring more settlers to Texas.

Spanish meaning
The word "empresario" is Spanish for "businessman."

EMPRESARIO

duties
- bring settlers to Texas
- set up communities
- uphold Mexican laws

what it is not
- government official
- woman
- Native American

Farming and ranching are still important to the Texas economy today.

MOSES AUSTIN STRIKES A DEAL

The empresario system of colonization began under the Spanish government. However, they chose only one empresario—Moses Austin. Austin had earned and lost a fortune mining lead in Missouri. In 1819, he came up with a plan to start an Anglo-American colony in Texas in order to escape his **debts**. In 1820, Austin traveled to San Antonio—the capital of Spanish Texas at the time. He asked Spanish officials for permission to start his colony there. The governor in charge accepted the plan, but it had to be accepted by Spanish authorities in Mexico City, too.

Austin had been working so hard on his plans that he didn't take good care of himself. The trip back to Missouri took 4 weeks. The weather was wet and cold, and he didn't eat well. By the time he reached his home, he was very ill.

Moses Austin was originally from Connecticut. He had been a businessman in Pennsylvania and Virginia before moving to Missouri.

statue of Moses Austin in San Antonio

13

STEPHEN AUSTIN TAKES OVER

Soon after arriving home, Moses Austin learned that the Spanish government had accepted his plan. He had permission to start a Texas colony with 300 Anglo-American families. However, he was not well enough to carry out his idea. Austin asked his son Stephen to complete his plan for colonization. Moses Austin died 2 days later on June 10, 1821.

Stephen had recently become a judge in Arkansas, but he left soon after to study law in New Orleans, Louisiana. When he heard about the deal his father had made for a colony in Texas, he didn't think it was a good idea. However, he decided to honor his father's wishes and move to Texas. Soon after his father died, Stephen Austin set out for San Antonio to check on his father's land grant.

In 1839, the Republic of Texas honored Stephen Austin by naming its new capital Austin. Today, Austin is the Texas state capital.

The Father of Texas

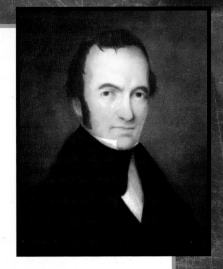

Stephen Austin was born in Virginia in 1793. He moved to Missouri with his family when he was 5. Stephen learned a lot about business from his father, Moses Austin. After going to college in Kentucky, Austin returned to Missouri to help run his father's lead-mining business.

Stephen Austin set up the first Anglo-American colony in Texas. During the Texas Revolution, he helped Texas win its independence from Mexico. He served as the new **republic's** first **secretary of state** until his death on December 27, 1836. Today, Stephen Austin is remembered as the "father of Texas."

On the way to San Antonio, Stephen Austin learned that Mexico had won its independence from Spain. Luckily for Austin, the Mexican government decided to continue the empresario system started by the Spanish. Once in San Antonio, he met with the new Mexican governor, who accepted Moses Austin's original plans.

After leaving San Antonio, Austin announced land for sale on the Brazos and Colorado rivers in east Texas. Interested colonists began arriving in December 1821. However, the governor of San Antonio soon told Austin that the Mexican government wasn't going to honor the deal after all. Austin traveled to Mexico City and convinced the Mexican government to grant him authority over the settlement. Although he had other problems with the government, Austin's settlement was a success.

This 1840 map was based on a map Stephen Austin had made before he died. It shows the land grants and colonies in Texas at the time.

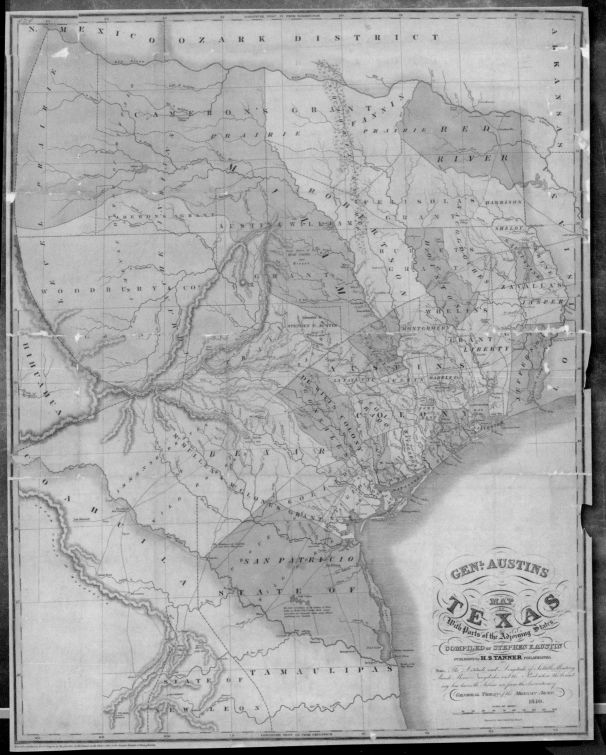

GENL. AUSTINS

MAP of TEXAS

With Parts of the Adjoining States

COMPILED BY STEPHEN F. AUSTIN

PUBLISHED BY H. S. TANNER Philadelphia

1840.

RISING POPULATION

Many Anglo-Americans were excited about the land offers from the Mexican government. Some wanted to buy cheap land and make money farming and raising cattle. Others, who had broken laws or owed money, used Texas as a place to hide from the U.S. government. The Mexican and U.S. governments had no agreements about returning people who had broken the law. So Americans could escape U.S. law by moving to Texas.

The Anglo-American colonists brought their own **cultures** and religious beliefs with them, and few wanted to give them up. They were used to doing things their own way and were sometimes unwilling to follow Mexican law. Many Texas colonists hoped that the United States—which was quickly expanding—would **annex** Texas, allowing them to become American citizens again.

Shown here is part of Stephen Austin's list of the "Old 300," a term that applies to the first Anglo-American families who settled in east Texas.

A Memorandum of Application

Names	When from	Date of Arrival	Date of Application
Kuykendall R. H. Electra his wife	Resident	Citizen	1st June 1835
J. Morton W. P.	Resident	Citizen	1st of June 1835
Powell John Dorcas his wife by his agent J. Stuart	Resident	Citizen	1st of June 1835
J. L. Richardson Sarah Ann his wife	Alabama February 1835	Not entitled to a league	1st of June 1835
David Hanson	Has a Certificate Resident Citizen		1st of June 1835
J. H. Fann Sarah his wife	Mississippi July 5th 1835	2nd of June 1835	
Peter T. Duncan Sally his wife	Ala. May 11th 1835	3 June 1835	
William Beasley Rachel his wife	Louisa Oct 1834	4 June 1835	
Charles Edwards by his agent J. Isenhoster	Ala Dec. 1834	4 June 1835	
Jesse Sutton	Miss May 1832	6 June 1835	
Joseph Bartlett	Resident Citizen	6 June 1835	
Robt. Brooks his wife	Mississippi May 1831	6 June 1835 has an old Certificate	
Wm. G. Evans his wife		1831 6 June 1835 Has a Certificate	
J. B. Travis agent — and will pay fees			

	Age			
Burk Trammell	26	Soltero		
... Ellen	34	Casado		
... zabeth Su muger	26			
...M. Coleman	33			
...zabeth Su muger	27	id	2	2
... Barksdale	26	Soltero		
... Coe	31			
...beth Su muger	18	Casado	1	3
...aniel Moore	53			
...ca Su muger	43	id		
...beth McConnell	21	Viudo		
...tus Williams	21	Soltero casado		
...y Su muger				
... Martin	27	id		
... Gill	28	id		
... Meentin	27	id		
... Brooks	23	Casado		
...m. Su muger	16			
...W. L. Hommedieu	28	Soltero		
... Lewis	31			
...muger	27	Casado	4	May...
... Pickens	23	id		
...Su muger	27	id	4	Labr...
...urnham	23	Soltero		
...M. Allen	25	id		

Although Stephen Austin proved to be the most successful empresario, others made similar contracts with the Mexican government. These men helped bring hundreds of settlers to Texas. The population grew quickly. Farms and cattle ranches also grew. Many settlers brought African **slaves** with them to work on their farms and ranches. The Mexican government was against slavery but often allowed it because of the money that came from farms and ranches with slaves.

As more colonists settled in Texas, the settlements grew closer together. Sometimes empresarios argued over land. In one case, the Mexican government had accidentally given the same piece of land to a Mexican-born empresario and an American-born empresario. The American was asked to move to a new area.

According to Mexican law, settlers were allowed to bring slaves they already owned. Slaves born in Texas were to be set free when they turned 14. The laws also banned slave trading. However, people often paid no attention to these laws.

Texas landowner watching slaves pick cotton

THE PATH TO TEXAS FREEDOM

When the young Mexican nation's **constitution** became law in 1824, Anglo-Americans were asked to take a **loyalty oath** to the new nation. Settlers were also expected to become Catholic if they weren't already. However, the Anglo-Americans in Texas practiced ways of life that were often very different from those in Mexico. Most Texans took the oath, but few wanted to change the way they lived and what they believed.

The people of Texas asked the new government of Mexico to grant them statehood. However, Mexican leaders chose to combine Texas with the area to the southwest to form the state of Coahuila (koh-ah-WEE-luh) and Texas. The capital was moved hundreds of miles away from the earlier capital in San Antonio. This made it even harder for people in Texas to have a voice in government.

This map from 1833 shows the state of Coahuila and Texas. The colored regions are land grants given to Anglo-American and Mexican settlers.

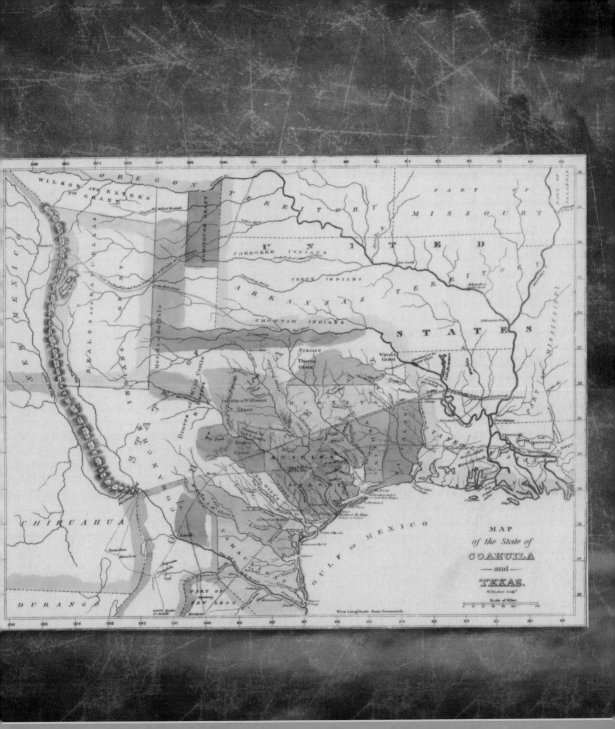

By the early 1830s, Anglo-American colonists had settled much of eastern Texas. The Mexican government was happy the area's population was growing. However, it worried about the steady increase in the number of Anglo-Americans. Many Anglo-Americans openly paid no attention to Mexican laws. Some even talked about independence. At the same time, the United States was quickly growing across North America. The Mexican government feared the United States wanted to annex Texas.

1871 Galveston, Texas

GALVESTON
TEXAS
1871

The Mexican government decided it must stop allowing Anglo-American colonists to enter Texas. It sent troops to patrol the northern border. It also put a new tax on goods coming from the United States, which hurt trade. People in Texas spoke out against Mexican trade laws.

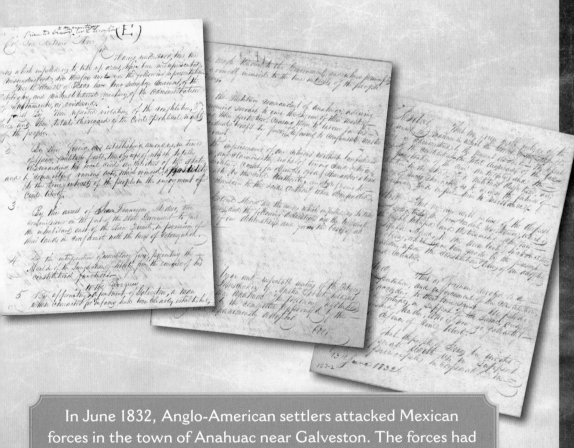

In June 1832, Anglo-American settlers attacked Mexican forces in the town of Anahuac near Galveston. The forces had been sent to make sure the settlers obeyed the trade laws. The settlers thought the trade laws were unfair. Later, the settlers wrote the Turtle Bayou Resolutions, shown here, to explain their reasons for attacking the Mexican forces at Anahuac.

In 1833, Anglo-American colonists in Texas wrote a letter to the Mexican government. They wanted Texas to become a state separate from Coahuila. Austin took the letter to Mexico City and presented it to the Mexican government. The government said no. It feared that Texans would now try to separate from Mexico, so officials quickly threw Austin in jail for 2 years.

When he was freed, Austin returned to Texas. He and other colonists knew that Texans would have to go to war to gain their freedom. The Texas Revolution began with the Battle of Gonzales in October 1835. Most of the battles were fought on land Texans had worked hard to settle and make their own. Texas won the war against Mexico in 1836 and became a free nation—the Republic of Texas.

This 1895 painting shows the Battle of San Jacinto, which was the final battle of the Texas Revolution. It was fought on April 21, 1836.

This painting shows Mexican general Antonio López de Santa Anna surrendering to Texas general Sam Houston after the Battle of San Jacinto. Houston is on the ground because he had been shot in the ankle during the battle.

BEYOND COLONIZATION

As many of the first Anglo-American settlers had hoped, the United States annexed Texas in 1845. It became the twenty-eighth U.S. state and had a population of about 100,000 people. Border disagreements between the United States and Mexico led to the Mexican-American War in 1846. Many Texans helped the United States win the war and move U.S. borders further south and west.

The Anglo-American colonists who originally settled in Texas were hardworking and self-sufficient. They were proud of their culture and ways of life. Texans have held on to these qualities. Today, they proudly honor the Anglo-American colonists who founded their great state.

The single star on the Texas state flag has long been a symbol of Texas. Texas is often called the Lone Star State.

U.S. History and Texas Colonization: A Timeline

UNITED STATES

TEXAS

UNITED STATES		TEXAS
[Ja]mes Monroe is elected to a second [te]rm as U.S. president.	**1820**	Moses Austin asks to establish an Anglo-American settlement in Texas.
[M]issouri becomes the twenty-fourth [U.]S. state.	**1821**	Anglo-American colonists begin settling in Texas.
	1823	Stephen Austin's land grant is officially recognized by Mexican government.
[A]ndrew Jackson wins popular [v]ote in presidential election, but [C]ongress declares John Quincy [A]dams the winner.	**1824**	The Mexican constitution becomes law but fails to grant Texas statehood.
[P]resident Andrew Jackson signs the [In]dian Removal Act into law.	**1830**	Mexico stops Anglo-American colonists from entering Texas.
[A]ndrew Jackson wins second term [a]s U.S. president.	**1832**	Texans attack Mexican fort in Anahuac, Texas.
	1835	Texas Revolution begins.
	1836	Texas wins the Texas Revolution and becomes a free nation.
[Ja]mes K. Polk becomes the eleventh [U.]S. president.	**1845**	Texas becomes the twenty-eighth U.S. state.

READER RESPONSE PROJECTS

- You are an empresario trying to get Anglo-Americans to move to Texas in 1820. Create a poster that will convince people to come.

- You are Stephen Austin. Your father has asked you to move to Texas. Write to him explaining why you don't think this is a good idea. Make sure you include the questions you have and your reasons for not wanting to go.

- You are an Anglo-American settler in Texas. Create a journal and make entries about what happens, what your life is like, and major events over the years. Include pictures.

GLOSSARY

annex (AA-nehks) To take over or add to.

Catholic (KATH-lihk) A person who belongs to the Roman Catholic Church.

constitution (kahn-stuh-TOO-shun) The basic rules by which a country or a state is governed.

culture (KUHL-chur) The beliefs, practices, and arts of a group of people.

debt (DEHT) Money owed to someone else.

economy (ih-KAH-nuh-mee) The production and use of goods and services in a community.

explorer (ihk-SPLOHR-uhr) Someone who travels and looks for new land.

frontier (fruhn-TIHR) The edge of a settled country, where the wilderness begins.

loyalty oath (LOY-uhl-tee OHTH) An official promise to obey the laws and beliefs of a group or country.

republic (rih-PUH-blihk) A form of government in which people vote for leaders who will make laws and run the government.

revolution (reh-vuh-LOO-shun) To overthrow or fight against the government in power.

secretary of state (SEH-kruh-tehr-ee UV STAYT) A government official in charge of a country's dealings with other countries.

slave (SLAYV) A person who is "owned" by another person and forced to work without getting paid.

INDEX

Due to the changing nature of Internet links, the Rosen Publishing Group, Inc., has developed an online list of Web sites related to the subject of this book. This site is updated regularly. Please use this link to access the list: **http://www.rcbmlinks.com/sot/angcol/**